I LOVE MY DAD

PRAISE FOR *I LOVE MY DAD*

Great Story!

This book stole my heart! The color-coded story is like training wheels for beginner readers, helping them ride the reading wave. It's bound to make them bookworms!
– travisc51

It's genius.
– Ms. Leitzel, English Special Education teacher

My Books

Genesis Solves Sumerian King List

Pharaohs of the Bible (4004 – 960 B.C.)

Pharaohs of the Bible (1003 B.C. – 70 A.D.)

Creator: His Story

Thorny Scriptures About Women

Biblical Answers to Abuse

American King James Bible: Old and New Testaments

American King James Bible and Founding Documents

and

I Love My Dad (also available on Audible)

I LOVE MY DAD

by A. Child

Inspired Idea Press

Prism Phonics' color-assonant text is based on patent 6126447 with a new patent pending.

Story Text Copyright © 1998, 2025 Eve Engelbrite

Colorized Text and Illustrations Copyright © 2025 Inspired Idea Press

Illustrations by Josephine Hampton

All rights reserved. No part of this publication may be reproduced, distributed, or transmitted in any form or by any means, including photocopying, recording, or other electronic or mechanical methods, without the prior written permission of the publisher, except as permitted by U.S. copyright law. For information on permissions, email: Contact@InspiredIdeaPress.com.

Rights to use Prism Phonics' color-assonant text are not for sale at this time. Www.PrismPhonics.com

"Scripture quotations from the (NASB®) New American Standard Bible®, Copyright © 2020 by The Lockman Foundation. Used by permission. All rights reserved. lockman.org"

Inspired Idea Press
P.O. Box 270183
Flower Mound, TX 75027
www.InspiredIdeaPress.com
Contact@InspiredIdeaPress.com

Printed in Coppell, TX

ISBN: 9781931203418

Library of Congress Control Number: 2025910764

INTRODUCTION

You are holding a unique "learn to read" book which includes the same illustrated story twice: first with Prism Phonics color-assonant text and last with standard black text. Only the vowel sounds are colored; therefore, the number of colors in a word equals the number of syllables in it. This single aspect is very helpful to new and struggling readers and those with dyslexia.

Color assonance means the same main vowel sound of the color is to be pronounced regardless of spelling. For example, "blue" contains the long /oo/ sound and can be spelled with 'o' as in 'to' or 'two', or 'oo' as in 'too', or 'u' as in 'flu', or 'ou' as in "through", or 'ue' as in 'glue', or 'ew' as in 'flew'. With color-assonant text new or struggling readers can learn to read without first having to learn spelling rules. The short /oo/ sound is often followed by a 'd' as in 'would' or 'wood' (homonyms) or by a 'k' as in 'book'. The 'r-controlled' and 'l-controlled' vowel sounds are both included in the color "purple" (which is a light tint to distinguish it from "plum"). Words ending with 'ng' or 'nk' heighten the placement of the preceding vowel like the /ih/ in "pink mint". If your region pronounces "orange" as /aw-ringe/, you might call it "mang*o*" instead. The key is two pages over The first five pages of the story include the color key, and then it goes away.

These are the normal sounds of the following consonants: 'c' is /k/, 'f' is /f/, 'g' is hard /g/, 'q' is /k/, 's' is /s/, 't' is /t/, 'x' is /ks/, and 'z' is /z/. Special consonant sounds are italicized.

I suggest the instructor (parent or teacher) read the first version of the story to the child using their finger underneath each word or phrase to indicate what they are reading. Then ask the learner to describe the picture. The second time the instructor should read the second version of the story with their finger gliding along in the same manner, but without stopping. The third and subsequent times, ask the learner which version of the story he/she wants. Some children are ready to learn to read at age 3, while others aren't ready until age 6 or 8 (sometimes due to delayed hearing or speech). When the learner requests the colorized text or asks about the vowels and consonants on the next two pages, they are indicating their readiness to learn.

Use the first version of the story and take turns reading the lines of colorized text with the instructor going first. That way the learner has the joy of repeating the title of the story. Teach the color names in the title. Ask the learner to point to the same color somewhere else on that page or in the story and pronounce the word and ask what was the same. Ask the learner to point to a consonant (black letter) in the title and the same consonant on that page; ask what was the same and what was different.

VOWELS

LONG

(says letter name: A, E, I, O, U)

GRA**Y**

GREE**N**

LI**ME**

ORA**N**G**E**

BLU**E**

OTHER

BROW**N**

TU**R**Q**U**OI**SE**

PUR**PL**E

SHORT

TA**N**

RE**D**

PI**NK**

BLO**ND**

PLU**M**

WOO**D**

based on patent 6126447 with new patent pending

SPECIAL CONSONANTS

c	city	/s/		s	has	/z/
	ocean	/sh/			treasure	/zh/
	cello	/ch/			sugar	/sh/
d	passed	/t/		t	nation	/sh/
	soldier	/j/			picture	/ch/
f	of	/v/			equation	/zh/
g	gym	/j/		x	exit	/gz/
	beige	/zh/			xylophone	/z/
q	plaque	/k/		z	azure	/zh/

ch	church	/ch/		wh - wheel	/hw/
	chute	/sh/		gh - laugh	/f/
sh - shop		/sh/		ph - phone	/f/
th	the	(voiced)		ng - sing	/ng/
	thin	(unvoiced)		nk - sink	/nk/
qu - queen		/kw/		sm - prism	/zum/

KEY:

Gray	Green	Lime	Orange	Blue	Brown	Turquoise
Tan	Red	Pink	Blond	Plum	Wood	Purple

This book is dedicated to my husband.

He has been instrumental in the development of Prism Phonics.

For decades he has championed my writing.

But most importantly, he is the "father" of this story.

I was blessed to observe all the beautiful moments

between father and son described in this story (though not in Mexico).

Happy Father's Day!

P.S. I placed a playground on the way to Parque México which is a
22-acre park featuring Art Deco architecture and fountains, ponds, and waterfalls.

Gray Green Lime   Orange Blue   Brown Turquoise
Tan   Red   Pink   Blond   Plum   Wood   Purple

Patting me,
Poking me,
Tickling me.
I love my Dad.

He puts me on his shoulders
And I can touch the ceiling.

| Gray | Green | Lime | Orange | Blue | Brown | Turquoise |
| Tan | Red | Pink | Blond | Plum | Wood | Purple |

He's better than a jungle gym.
I sure love him.

| Gray | Green | Lime | Orange | Blue | Brown | Turquoise |
| Tan | Red | Pink | Blond | Plum | Wood | Purple |

I take a ride upon his foot.
And walk between his legs.

I spy *things* on the ground for him;
He tells me how *they*'re made.

There's the park.
I like to swing
And play with kids.
And . . .

Dad holds my hand to cross *the* street;
I break away to run.

He catches me and tells me "No". No park today; no fun.

And yet I feel so safe somehow
When we go for a walk.
And I love him even more
For taking time to talk.

| Gray | Green | Lime | Orange | Blue | Brown | Turquoise |
| Tan | Red | Pink | Blond | Wood | Plum | Purple |

Science facts,
Tongue twisters,
Funny jokes.
I love my Dad.

**Bible stories,
Song rhymes,
Good times.
I love my Dad.**

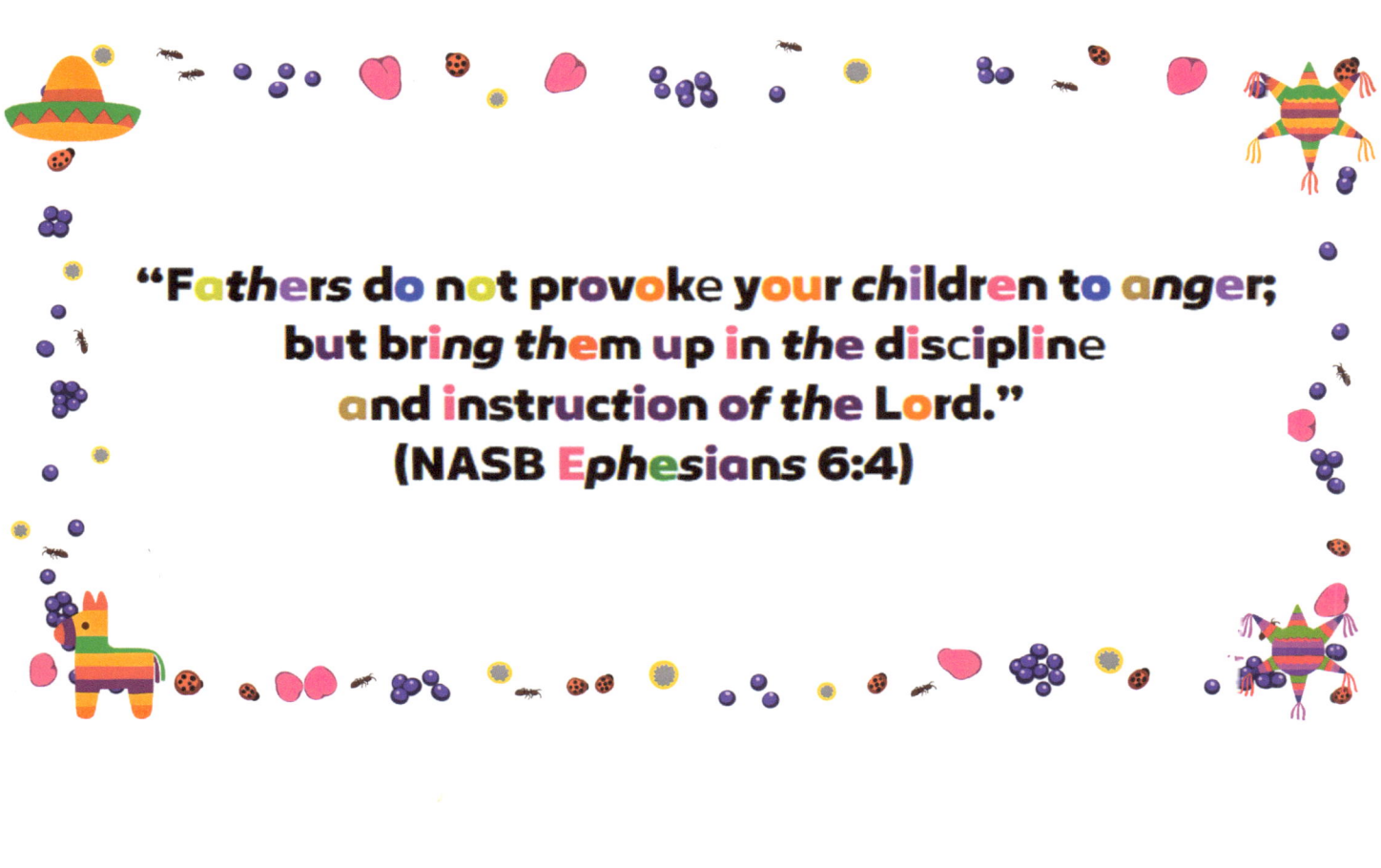

"Fathers do not provoke your children to anger; but bring them up in the discipline and instruction of the Lord."
(NASB Ephesians 6:4)

I LOVE MY DAD

(in regular, black text)

by A. Child

Hugging me,
Holding me,
Squeezing me.
I love my Dad.

He's better than a jungle gym.
I sure love him.

I take a ride upon his foot. And walk between his legs.

Green grass,
Brown bugs,
Pink petals,
I love my Dad.

Bottle cap,
Pretty rock,
Ladybug.
I love my Dad.

There's the park.
I like to swing
And play with kids.
And . . .

And yet I feel so safe somehow
When we go for a walk.
And I love him even more
For taking time to talk.

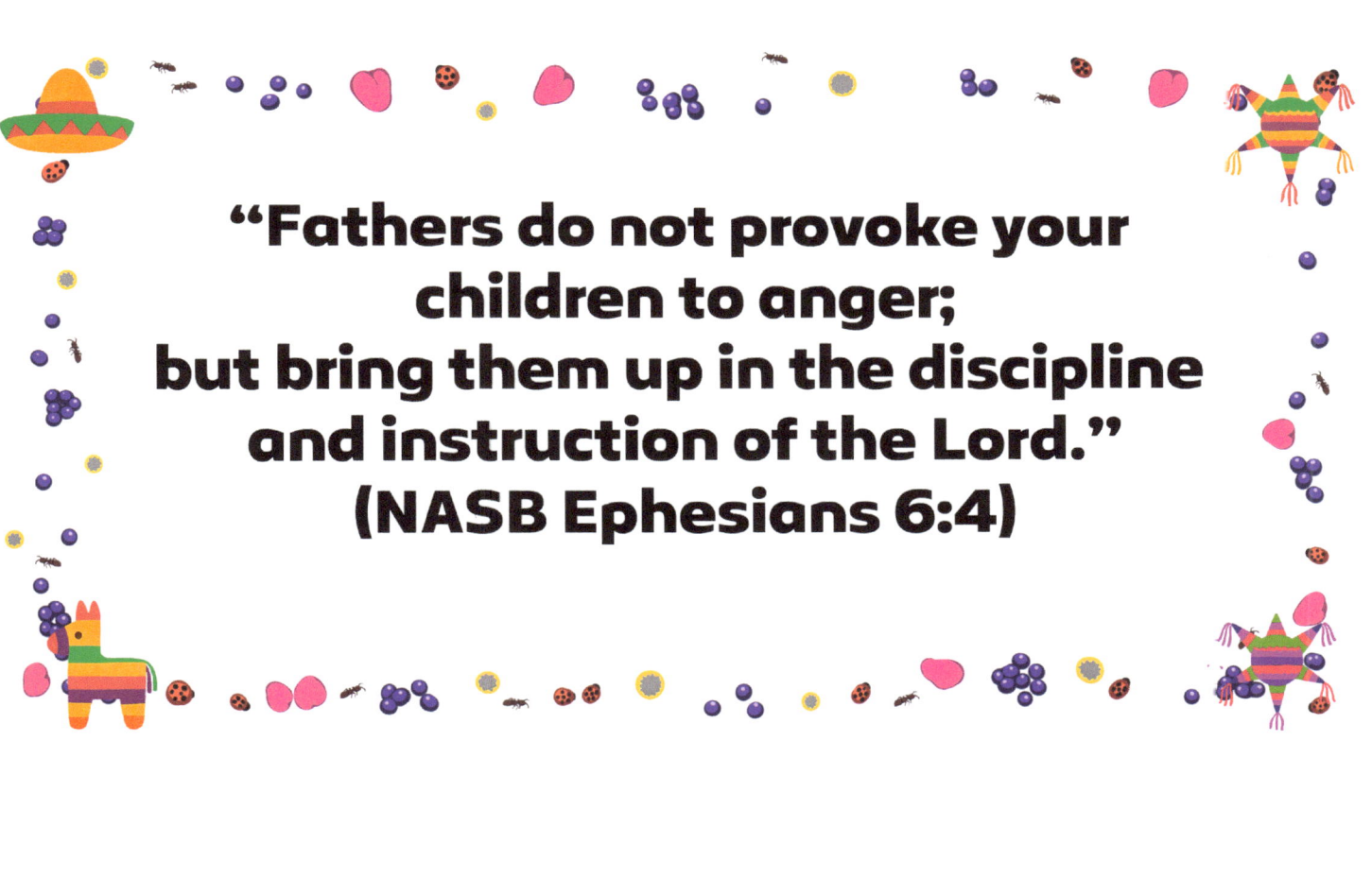

"Fathers do not provoke your children to anger;
but bring them up in the discipline and instruction of the Lord."
(NASB Ephesians 6:4)

ME AND MINE

The son in this story is 4-years old which was an important age for my son. He was wanting to learn to read, but I was not satisfied with the comprehensive phonetic reading programs available in the 90's. I used "Sing, Spell, Read, and Write" with him, but I also began to develop my own with the amazing help of my husband and his team. It became the software product "Color Phonics". Brief videos instructed how to create each of the 43 phonemes of American English. Then aural tests (ear training) to differentiate the most common sounds occurred in a game format. Color Phonics taught 46 spelling patterns, over 850 "Sound-It-Out" blends, and recognition of over 1,300 words within 33 stories all on 5 CD's. The product sold well and many people wrote saying now they could read. At that time color printing was too expensive to print books with colorized text, but now it's not.

After a few improvements and a new name for the old system, the colorized text will continue to assist pronunciation and reading. I and others would like to read your feedback.
PLEASE WRITE A REVIEW!

Back then I had my young son use 14 colored pencils specific to the color-assonant vowel sounds to color the vowels in his readers. This helped him see the different ways the same vowel sound was spelled in various words. I have developed PDF files of the text of the stories with the vowels in outline form to be colored. Go to www.prism-phonics.com to purchase them.